Original title:
Christmas Hopes and Hearthside Dreams

Copyright © 2024 Creative Arts Management OÜ
All rights reserved.

Author: Riley Hawthorne
ISBN HARDBACK: 978-9916-94-036-5
ISBN PAPERBACK: 978-9916-94-037-2

Fireside Stories and Timeless Tales

Gather 'round, we've tales anew,
Of socks that vanish and stew that flew.
A cat in a hat and a dog with glee,
They danced on the table, just wait and see.

Grandma's pie, a sight to behold,
Spiced with love, and stories retold.
But hold your breath, don't take a bite,
It might just giggle and take flight tonight.

Radiance of Friendship and Feasts

Friends arrive with hug and cheer,
Bringing goodies and laughter near.
A turkey that quacked, what a surprise,
It strutted about with bright, gleaming eyes.

Laughter sparkles like fairy lights,
As mishaps unfold on these cozy nights.
Watch the jello wiggle with magic flair,
A wobbly treat ends up everywhere!

When Hope Glimmers in the Chill

The chill in the air brings warmth within,
We sip hot cocoa, let the giggles begin.
A snowman with socks and a carrot so sly,
He waves at the penguins who stroll by.

When socks go missing, it's pure delight,
A rogue laundry gnome must be in sight.
But we laugh as we dream and chew on bread,
Imagining what other nonsense is spread.

Hearthside Whispers Beneath the Stars

Beneath the stars, there's laughter galore,
As marshmallows plump like never before.
A raccoon steals cookies, what a foul thief,
But we just laugh, it gives us relief.

Sipping hot cider, we whisper and scheme,
With silly wishes that float like a dream.
"Let's build a snow fort that's ten feet tall!"
As snowflakes tumble, we have a ball.

Sledding Down the Slopes of Dreams

Sledding down the hills so steep,
I fly like a bird, not a sheep.
With laughter bouncing in the air,
I spy a snowman without a care.

A wobbly ride brings giggles galore,
We crash and tumble, wanting more.
Hot cocoa waits, but first, oh dear!
I lose my hat and start to cheer!

Warm Snuggles in the Coldest of Nights

Under blankets, we pile so tight,
Rhymes and stories bring pure delight.
With pillows like clouds and dreams like cake,
Who'd guess I snore like a wide-awake snake?

The cat joins in, a furry ball,
In our snuggly fortress, we all stand tall.
Hot chocolate spills with a marshmallow dive,
It's a giggly mess, but we feel alive!

Tucked in Dreams Beneath the Covers

Tucked in tight with a story or two,
I dream of dragons, and tacos too!
Each flip of the page, a new silly scene,
Where everything's weird and nothing is mean.

Beneath my blanket, adventures awake,
I find a unicorn that loves to bake.
He makes chocolate cakes that fly like a bird,
With sprinkles and giggles, it's perfectly absurd!

The Magic of Wishes Spun in Light

Twinkling lights dance on the tree,
As wishes float like soft poetry.
I wish for slippers that grow on my feet,
And socks that sparkle—now that's a treat!

The ornaments chat, they giggle and grin,
Telling tales of where they've been.
Each twirl of the star spins joy to the night,
And every last wish takes glorious flight!

Messages of Friendship in the Air

We gather round with snacks galore,
Laughter spills from every door.
Eggnog spills, and cookies dance,
Who knew that friends could be such a chance?

With mismatched socks and silly hats,
We share our tales of all our spats.
A snowman's grin melts into cheer,
Or maybe it's just too much beer!

Embracing the Season's Soft Glow

The lights are twinkling, oh so bright,
As cats pounce on the tree at night.
Ornaments dropped, a crashing sound,
We sing off-key but spread joy around.

Grandma's cookies are a tad too sweet,
A sugar rush that's hard to beat.
With funny sweaters and goofy grins,
Let the games and joyous mayhem begin!

Magical Moments in a Winter Wonderland

Snowflakes swirl like a wild ballet,
While Uncle Joe's lost his way.
He's tangled in lights from head to toe,
As we can't stop laughing at the show!

The snowball fight is fierce and bright,
Launching fluff with all our might.
Then inside the warm, cozy nook,
We spill hot cocoa on the good book!

Dancing Shadows and Frost-Kissed Laughter

The shadows dance as shadows do,
While the cat plots mischief anew.
It knocks the fruitcake off the shelf,
Now it's a game for the whole elf!

With a flurry of giggles and warm delight,
We roast marshmallows, oh what a sight!
The fire crackles, the stories flow,
As we wink at ghosts from long ago!

Lanterns of Love in the Night

The candles flicker, shadows dance,
A cat jumps up, a squirrel's chance.
Uncle Joe spills eggnog on his shirt,
The cookies vanish, oh, what a flirt!

Lights twinkle high, and socks are stuffed,
Grandma's sweet fudge, all homemade, puffed.
The tree looks splendid, crooked it's true,
Yet somehow, it shines like morning dew.

Joyful Gatherings around the Flame

Gathered 'round with laughter loud,
A roast explodes, we cheer the crowd.
Cousin Tim's dancing, two left feet,
While Aunt Mae's cooking up something sweet.

The fire's crackling, popcorn flies,
Someone's dragging home the prize.
A toast to fun, with mugs held high,
It's hard to keep our spirits dry.

The Spirit of Giving and Grateful Hearts

Wrapped in paper, gifts piled tall,
Surprises await, will someone fall?
The puppy digs a hole in the box,
While grandpa snores, cuddled with the flocks.

In the spirit of sharing, we take a bite,
Of mystery dishes, oh, what a sight!
With belly laughs and joyful cheers,
We'll savor jests through all our years.

Festive Dreams Wrapped in Tinsel

Tinsel sparkles, lights aglow,
Dad's up high, singing hello.
Ornaments swing on a tree so grand,
The dog tries hard to make a stand.

We hang wishes, bold and bright,
As the snowflakes whirl, a pure delight.
With cheer that echoes, and spirits high,
Oh, what fun to just let fly!

Murmurs of Hope in the Chill

Frosty air, a squirrel's delight,
Finding nuts in the dead of night.
Laughter sneaks through cracks so wide,
As snowmen plot and parents hide.

Chimney smoke swirls like a dance,
While kids slip in a daring prance.
Mittens tossed like confetti bright,
Their laughter echoes, pure delight.

A Symphony of Embers and Echoes

Sizzle crackles, popcorn flies,
In the flicker of warm goodbyes.
Barking dogs, they join the fun,
As strange gifts turn to a good pun.

Grandma's chair creaks with a cheer,
As relatives share tales sincere.
A mishap with some eggnog spills,
Laughter erupts, we've got the thrills!

Solstice Light and Hearthstone Comforts

Candles flicker, casting shadows bold,
While silly stories from grandpa unfold.
Hats made of tinsel, jingle bells jive,
While in the corner, a cat comes alive.

Ornaments hang with a twist and a spin,
As we debate if we're winning or chagrin.
A dance-off erupts under mistletoe,
With Auntie's moves so delightfully slow.

Nostalgic Aromas in the Air

Gingerbread scents fill the space,
With icing that looks like a funny face.
Parade of snacks, their flavors unite,
As uncles try baking with all of their might.

Oh, turkey's burned, and whoops, that pie!
But joy sprinkles laughter, oh me, oh my!
With goofy hats and festive cheer,
As we toast, we know good times are here!

A Song of Stars and Serenity

In the sky, twinkling lights play,
They wink at us, hip-hip-hooray!
Snowflakes dance with a jolly twist,
Even Santa joins, he can't resist.

Cookies gone, what a sneaky feat,
Rudolph munching on leftover treats.
Elves at the workshop, full of cheer,
But they forgot who wrapped that weird deer.

Hot cocoa spills, oops, what a splash,
Marshmallows float, it's quite the clash!
Chasing kittens 'round the old tree,
A holiday scene, who's laughing with glee?

Stars above with a giggle bright,
Sleigh bells jingle in the moonlight.
Joyful antics, what a happy scene,
With laughter echoing, we're all so keen.

The Hearth's Gentle Embrace

By the fire, we snuggle real tight,
With socks full of holes, oh what a sight!
The cat on the mantel thinks he's the king,
As we side-eye the last piece of zing.

Nuts cracking loud, we jump and shout,
Who knew peanuts could create such doubt?
Bobby burned the pie, oh dear me,
Now we feast on a lump of tree.

Lights flicker bright, a comedic show,
Caught in a tangle, oh where did they go?
The stockings are hung, but wait, what's that?
A sock full of jellybeans — how about that?

Mirthful moments, oh how they gleam,
The hearth glowing softly, a cozy dream.
With every chuckle and silly cheer,
We toast to the warmth of loved ones near.

Glimmers of Joy Amidst the Frost

Snowmen wobble with cheeky grins,
Three carrot noses, where do we begin?
A snowball fight up on the hill,
But don't throw hard, or you might spill!

Frosty windows tell tales of yore,
Of how Grandma danced and fell on the floor.
With gingerbread crumbs stuck on our face,
A cookie warrior's sweet, sugary grace.

Eggnog spills — that's quite the sight,
Cheers to the mishaps that bring pure delight!
Elf hats are worn in the strangest way,
Just a regular night gone totally astray.

Outside it's chilly, yet inside we glow,
Wrapped up in chaos, just lettin' it flow.
As laughter echoes from the floor to the beams,
We cherish the night, filled with whimsical dreams.

Evergreens and Enchanted Evenings

The tree's leaning, oh what a fall,
With lights misbehaving, they need to install.
Star on the top, slightly askew,
But who really cares, it's just me and you!

Tinsel fights are the best kind of fun,
Though Dad always says, 'Next year we're done!'
Ornaments clink as they tumble down,
Mom's rolling her eyes with a goofy frown.

Mistletoe hangs, but oh wait, what's this?
A cheeky puppy thinks it's a game to kiss!
With laughter and giggles, we lean in for more,
Under the boughs, who could ask for a score?

As candles flicker with a warm fuzzy light,
We swap silly stories deep into the night.
With hearts full of joy, we all sway and sway,
Wishing for this fun to never decay!

Dreams Adrift on Snowy Breezes

On frosty nights, we chase a dream,
With snowflakes dancing, a silly theme.
A reindeer wearing socks so warm,
And visions of a candy storm.

Laughter echoing through the air,
As snowmen wobble, unaware.
The dog in boots, a sight to see,
Chasing flakes like they're meant to be.

From rooftops brightly decked with care,
To tangled lights that glimmer, flare.
We bundle up like giant muffs,
Giggling softly, calling bluffs.

So let's release a silly cheer,
For laughter shared with those held dear.
The dreams that drift on winter's breath,
Are wrapped in joy, and not in depth.

Treasures in the Glow of Togetherness

Gather 'round the twinkling lights,
Tales of mischief, giggles, and flights.
The cat, confused by every cheer,
Claiming each box without a fear.

Grandma's cookies, slightly burnt,
Yet every bite is warm, not terse.
Unwrapping gifts with wild delight,
Socks again? Oh, what a sight!

Tinsel tangled in our hair,
As we dance without a care.
Funny faces made for fun,
Togetherness, our number one.

So raise a mug of gooey brew,
To treasures found in laughs anew.
With hearts aglow, let's make a pact,
To cherish every silly fact.

Mirth Beneath the Pine

Underneath the tree so bright,
We swap our jokes, out of sheer delight.
A pickle hidden, oh what a thrill,
The quest for laughter never still.

Fuzzy socks and hats askew,
As we fashion snowmen, just a few.
A boisterous giggle in the night,
Presents flying, what a sight!

With twinkling eyes and hearts on fire,
We stoke the warmth, build dreams higher.
In every corner, merriment reigns,
For joy and laughter are our gains.

So gather 'round, let's share the cheer,
For underneath this pine, it's clear.
The moments shared, the smiles that gleam,
Are treasures found in every dream.

The Pillow of December's Embrace

Oh, cozy pillow, soft and round,
In your fluff, warm thoughts abound.
With winter tales and cocoa dreams,
We wrap ourselves in silly schemes.

The world outside, a frosty play,
As we snicker, then drift away.
A blanket fort, our kingdom bright,
Where nonsense reigns throughout the night.

Decorating hats made for squirrels,
A giggling fit, as chaos swirls.
In every smile, the warmth persists,
As dreams frolic in snowy mists.

So clutch your pillow, squeeze it tight,
For snug embraces spark our light.
With laughter filling winter's space,
We find a home in December's grace.

Enchanted Moments by the Fire

With marshmallows dancing high,
And Uncle Joe's loud, snore-filled sighs,
The logs crackle in a cozy tone,
As shadows do the cha-cha alone.

The dog snags all the tasty treats,
While grandpa's in his festive sweats.
Fairy lights twinkle, softer than sighs,
As we plot how to prank Auntie wise.

Hot cocoa spills like winter's cheer,
As giggles bounce off the pine-needle sphere.
Each moment a snapshot, a snow-globe tease,
Filled with laughter, and memories to freeze.

So here's to the nights, warm and bright,
Where silly stories take lofty flight.
By the fire, we share our silly schemes,
In these enchanted moments of frosted dreams.

Snowflakes and Heartfelt Embraces

The snowflakes fall like sprinkles of fun,
While giggling kiddos dash and run.
They tumble, trip, and barrel roll,
Yelling, 'Watch out!', a sight to behold.

Mom's out front, forming a snowman,
With a hat too big and a quirky plan.
He winks at me with buttoned eyes,
Just wait till he reads the frosty skies.

Dad's in the kitchen, burning the bread,
'It's toast with flair!' he says, turning red.
We laugh and sip our drinks so sweet,
With smiles that make this moment complete.

With snowballs flung amidst all the cheer,
Small touches of love fill the atmosphere.
Each frosty breath whispers tales untold,
Of joyful escapades in memories bold.

The Magic of Candlelit Evenings

Candlelight gleams on Dad's bald head,
As shadows dance and hearts are fed.
A flickering spark, a soft, warm glow,
As we try not to steal the last s'more, though.

Mom sings out of tune, what a treat,
While the cat plots to steal my seat.
We giggle at the starlit scene,
With humor bright as a tinsel sheen.

A game of charades, oh what a blunder,
With each gesture full of festive wonder.
We stumble and trip, a comedic parade,
As the candle flickers, no moment delayed.

These evenings glow like a sweet refrain,
Full of laughter, love, and a touch of insane.
Each flicker a memory waiting to be found,
In the magic of evenings where joy is unbound.

Sledding Through Starry Wishes

Down the hill, we make our way,
With sleds that tumble, oh what a display!
Each whoop and holler, a comet's flight,
As snowflakes turn our cheeks all white.

There goes Tommy, arms in the air,
Flipping like a pro, without a care.
We land in a pile, all giggles and noise,
Building dreams from the chaos of boys.

Mom yells out, 'Stay clear of that tree!',
While we giggle and plan our next spree.
The stars above, our guiding lights,
As we sled through the magic of winter nights.

So here's to the thrills, the laughter, the cheer,
To starry wishes, and hot cocoa near.
With friends by our side, tangles we'll weave,
In this wonderland that we never want to leave.

The Circle of Family and Firelight

Gather round with mugs in hand,
Where stories weave like grains of sand.
A cat in a hat, a dog in boots,
They join our feast, demanding my roots.

The uncle cracks jokes that barely land,
While Auntie rolls eyes, her patience spanned.
Laughter erupts like a popped balloon,
The fire flickers; we'll be up soon.

Mismatched socks from a gift exchange,
The game of charades gets oddly strange.
Grandma's casserole, a sight to behold,
Tastes like socks but is served with gold.

As the night winds down, we sing out of tune,
In the glow of the fire, joy's our monsoon.
If chaos is bliss, we've found our way,
In this circle of love, we joyfully stay.

Visions of Joy in the Network of Twinkles

Lights on the tree flicker and sway,
Grandpa's snoring steals the show today.
The tinsel fights static, it's quite a show,
While kids play hide-and-seek, go, go, go!

The cookies are burnt, yet smiles abound,
A jolly mishap; the best taste found.
In a tangle of ribbons, we share a laugh,
Oh, the glitter of mishaps—our photographic gaffe!

Mom's secret recipe, a funny old tale,
Thick as a brick, do we need more ale?
When laughter's the feast, who needs dessert?
With a wink and a grin, it's all we assert.

Underneath the twinkles, we raise a cheer,
For moments like these bring our hearts near.
In this web of delight, forever we'll weave,
Our shimmering stories on this wondrous eve.

A Haven Where Hearts Align

Amidst the fuss of wrapping and bows,
We gather with giggles, that's how it goes.
Slipper socks worn with pride and glee,
Each twist of the yarn, a tale to see.

Presents zigzag like cats on a spree,
While kids bicker; could it be just me?
The mayhem unfolds with each festive cheer,
As laughter and chaos draw us all near.

Mom's fond of dressing in her holiday flair,
Dad's jokes fly like marshmallows in air.
When we gather 'round, good vibes we deploy,
A snug little circus of warmth and joy.

In this cozy nook, our hearts dance and sing,
We share in the fun that laughter can bring.
So here's to the moments that make us shine,
In this haven of warmth, our spirits align.

Revelries Wrapped in Cozy Quilts

Under a quilt, piled high with cheer,
The fireplace crackles, our jokes fill the air.
A dance-off erupts in our makeshift space,
With the dog barking loud, adding to the pace.

The cocoa spills, oh what a sight!
As we stumble through games late into the night.
Sisters tease brothers, who play the fool,
In this merry madness, love's the golden rule.

The sliding of gifts brings a clatter of glee,
With one named for Dad, it's a joke, can't you see?
His face turns red, a sight to behold,
It's really a hammer, gift-wrapped in gold.

From giggles and smiles to whimsical dreams,
In this cozy quilt, life's not what it seems.
We celebrate together, all wrapped up tight,
In revelries radiant, till morn's early light.

Echoes of Laughter by the Flames

In the glow of the fire, we gather round,
Telling tales of the year, with giggles abound.
Not a creature is stirring, just a cat in a hat,
As we ponder the gifts, like weird socks and that.

The cookies are missing; who ate all the treats?
The dog's got the evidence, crushed on his feet.
With each silly story, we laugh and we cheer,
Pooling our blunders, all cozy right here.

A Gentle Tiding of Dreams

Whispers of dreams float high in the air,
While Uncle Joe snores in his old armchair.
The elves are conspiring, the reindeer too,
As we hide surprise gifts, oh what will they do?

With snowflakes a-fallin' and lights soft and bright,
We argue 'bout who has the best holiday lights.
The dog's in the corner, he joined in the fun,
Chasing after a ball, oh what have we spun!

Wrapped in Warmth, Wrapped in Love

The chilly air bites, but we're snug in our clothes,
With blankets and hot cocoa, the laughter just grows.
A knitting disaster, we cackle and tease,
As we fashion a scarf that looks like Swiss cheese.

Each gift that we share brings a grin and a cheer,
Even Grandma's fruitcake, we all still revere.
With cookies and stories, the evening won't end,
Just a wild band of misfits, each one a dear friend!

The Spirit of Giving Beneath Velvet Skies

Under twinkling stars, we all gather near,
With laughter like sleigh bells, and warmth in our cheer.
The snowman is melting; oh what a disgrace,
We might need a snowman to lighten our pace!

We wrap up our wishes in ribbons and bows,
Like gifting the cat with the prettiest clothes.
With funny surprises and giggles galore,
We dance by the fire, and who could want more?

Radiant Hearts Under the Mistletoe

In the kitchen, cookies burn,
Gifts under the tree take a turn.
A cat sprawls on the tinsel bright,
Dreaming of fish in the soft, night light.

Uncle Bob dons his Santa gear,
While Auntie giggles with too much cheer.
The dog steals a snack off the plate,
Now he's plotting, it's gonna be great!

Mistletoe hung by the door frame,
Cousins sneak in to play a game.
Lipstick marks and laughter loud,
'Twas supposed to be a quiet crowd!

Eggnog spills on the happy floor,
"Who spilled this?" comes a curious roar.
But laughter fills the air tonight,
As we embrace the silly delight.

Frosty Tales Around the Fire

Gathered 'round with steaming cups,
We tell tales of mishaps and hiccup ups.
Grandpa says he once lost his shoe,
On a slippery path—oh, what a view!

The snowman we made, a funny sight,
With a carrot nose that gave a fright.
He melted fast, but left behind,
Warm memories that twinkle and blind.

The raccoon came, seeking sweet pie,
We shooed him away but oh, how he'd try!
With paws so nimble and snacks in tow,
He danced with joy in the soft, white glow.

Laughter ignites like flames so bright,
Each story shared brings pure delight.
In this cozy nook, with joy we weave,
Funny moments are what we believe.

Illumination in Winter's Grip

The lights are twinkling, but somewhat askew,
A squirrel's moved in—not just any, but two.
They plan a parade on the power line,
As we sip hot cocoa, feeling divine.

The carolers knock, then start to sing,
But one forgot words— its quite the fling!
With giggles and oops, they all lose track,
Now they're trapped in a harmonical smack!

Frosty breath in the chilly air,
With snowflakes swirling, we run without care.
Yet slips and falls become a new song,
We laugh at the awkward—come join us along!

So as they cheer and icicles glint,
Victory dances with joy—what a hint!
In this twisty season, where joy's the aim,
We play like children, relishing the game.

Joy's Tapestry in a Woolen Frame

Patchwork sweaters all mismatched,
Knitting needles clicking, yarn attached.
Grandma's barking, "Knit faster, please!"
While Grandpa snoozes with a grin that frees.

The stockings are stuffed but oh what a sight,
Filled with odd trinkets that spark delight.
A toy from last year, half-melted too,
Confuses us all—what's a child to do?

We wrap ourselves in a cozy quilt,
As family stories spill like milk spilt.
Each one a treasure, stitched with care,
They brighten this season, beyond compare.

With laughter and cheer, we toast the night,
To mismatched socks and sheer delight.
For when we gather, the warmth we share,
Brings forth the magic of love in the air.

The Art of Nesting in Winter's Embrace

When snowflakes fall and cheeks turn red,
We pile up pillows in the warmest bed.
With snacks galore and laughter in the air,
Our little nest feels like a cozy lair.

The cat curls up, a furry little blob,
While outside, the neighbors are on a sob.
We sip hot cocoa, watch the world snowball,
That's the beauty of winter, after all!

Fluffy blankets wrapped around our feet,
Who needs a throne? This chair's a treat!
Hunting for socks that sort of match,
With mismatched slippers, we need a new patch.

So raise your mugs for the cozy nights,
The laughter and snacks, the snowball fights.
Nesting's an art that we hold dear,
With winter's embrace, we spread the cheer!

Strands of Joysen and the Flickering Flame

With twinkling lights all strung around,
We're hoping for fun, not just profound.
The cat's chasing shadows under the tree,
While we laugh till we can barely see!

The fireplace crackles, the marshmallows toast,
Telling wild tales that our friends love most.
One's dressed like an elf, another like a reindeer,
In the gallery of laughter, joy's the souvenir.

Sipping our drinks, we make silly cheers,
With rich, melted chocolate that conquers fears.
In the glow of the hearth, we all start to sway,
Dancing our troubles and worries away!

So gather around, let the stories be told,
As the night grows older and laughter's bold.
With joysen strands and flickering flame,
We freeze our worries and ignite our game!

Naturals Wonders Beneath Winter's Veil

A snowman stands with a carrot for a nose,
Though it's common, he strikes a funny pose.
With buttons like coal and a scarf that's bright,
His fashion sense is questionable—what a sight!

The flurries dance, then decide to play,
While I attempt to shovel, go astray.
The broomstick's swaying, I'm dodging the snow,
With each clumsy move, I'm putting on a show!

Ice skating dreams that meet the frost,
At the end of the day, who cares if I'm lost?
My friends are here to tumble and twirl,
With giggles and laughter, life's quite a whirl!

Under winter's veil, we find the fun,
With snowball wars until the day is done.
The wonders of nature, we playfully invoke,
Winter's charm reveals with every poked joke!

Miracles Found in Wrapped Moments

As gifts stack high, wrapped bows and tape,
The mystery builds, oh, what shape!
We guess and giggle, what could it be?
A partridge in a pear or just some old tea?

Sniffing the air, we start to unwrap,
A sock, a hat, or maybe a map?
With every layer, the fun levels rise,
In this family circus, there's joy in disguise!

Each moment we share is a gift itself,
More precious than any toy on a shelf.
So let's raise a toast with leftover cake,
Miracles abound in every mistake!

From ribbons and wrappings, to laughter and love,
We find that the gifts come from above.
In this time of cheer, let's dance and hop,
Wrapped moments of joy that never do stop!

Whispers of Yuletide Wishes

On rooftops reindeer do a dance,
While kids find time to take a chance.
They write to Santa, oh so bold,
Their letters spill secrets, fun to be told.

Gingerbread men, they start to flee,
From sticky fingers, as if to agree.
With frosting smiles, they laugh and cheer,
As milk's left out, and cookie cups leer.

Mistletoe hangs, but watch out for that,
Avoid the awkward, or maybe a spat.
With giggles and chuckles, all is in play,
Just don't slip on snow—what a funny day!

So gather around, let stories ignite,
With laughter and warmth, we banish the night.
For in every corner, with joy we deem,
Cherished retellings create our dream.

Beneath the Evergreen Canopy

Under the tree where mischief brews,
The cat's on the lights, chasing bright hues.
Tinsel's twinkling, but not quite right,
As Fido tries to join in the night.

Stockings hung, all filled with fun,
Expectations rise, it's just begun.
Who needs a sleigh when you've got a zip?
Dad's on the roof, with his dubious grip.

Cocoa spills while laughter streams,
Marshmallows bounce like tiny dreams.
Mom's trying to cook, but what a sight,
With flour on her nose, it's pure delight!

So toast to the fun, with wine in hand,
As family shenanigans surely expand.
For under the branches, so cozy, so bright,
Cherished memories make every heart light.

Threads of Light in Darkened Hours

As night falls down with a shimmering gaze,
The lights twinkle on in a wondrous maze.
In the chaos of wrapping, a mishap ensues,
The cat's in the box, and the dog's got the shoes.

Socks meant for gifts, end up on the floor,
With socks for the kids and snacks at the door.
The kids giggle hard, at the chaos they see,
As we try to wrangle their energy spree.

Twinkling bulbs and laughter resound,
When Uncle Joe starts dancing around.
In outrageous sweaters that practically glow,
With every twirl it's a silly show!

So gather your loved ones, crank up the cheer,
With stories and giggles, let's bring the good beer.
For all of these moments, both silly and bright,
Are threads that we cherish, through the longest night.

Cocoa and Comfort by Candlelight

With mugs full of cocoa, warm and divine,
We cozy up close, and everything's fine.
The marshmallows float, like clouds in the sky,
While Dad starts to sip—oh, how time does fly!

In pajamas that match, we gather 'round,
As we share the stories where laughter is found.
Spilled on the couch, a crumb makes its plea,
Watch out for the cat—she's eyeing the spree!

Candles flicker low with a cheerful glare,
As goofy old jokes float up in the air.
Mom's classic line: 'Don't eat that so fast!'
But who can resist? The joy is a blast!

So raise your mug high, let's toast to the night,
With comfort and warmth, everything feels right.
For laughter and cocoa, we hold so dear,
Create the warm memories we love all year.

Whispers of Winter Warmth

In a blanket so thick, with a cocoa so rich,
I ponder the antics that come with the pitch.
The cat on the mantel, a king on his throne,
Claims all of the cushions—he's set all alone.

With mittens for hands, I search for the treats,
Hidden by snowflakes, a wintertime feat.
My scarf starts to tangle, I laugh at the sight,
'Tis a fashion disaster, oh what a delight!

The snowmen are grinning, with carrots for noses,
Yet one took a tumble—oh, winter exposes!
I chuckle and build him a buddy named Bob,
Now both look quite silly, a true winter job.

As frost bites my toes, the fireplace roars,
My socks look like creatures escaping old drawers.
The warmth of the glow, it melts all my fears,
And dances bring laughter, through chilly night years.

Flickering Lights and Silent Nights

The twinkling lights seem to laugh in the dark,
Hiding behind trees like glowworms in park.
I trip on the cord, oh what a fine show,
My dance with the shadows? A sight to bestow!

Eggnog spills over—oops, there goes my plan,
The cookies were stellar, all made by the man.
But now they're not round, like a Christmas surprise,
More like little moons with some very sad eyes!

Those carolers outside, a hilarious crew,
Singing off-key, just like we always do.
But there's joy in the blunders, the giggles they bring,
In a chorus of goofs, we all start to sing!

With laughter and warmth, we gather around,
Each story a treasure, each chuckle profound.
In this chaos of cheer, by the glow of the night,
We find all our joys in the laughter so bright.

The Gift of Glowing Embers

The fire crackles softly, it pops with delight,
But so do the marshmallows, oh, what a sight!
I reach for the s'mores, they tumble and fall,
Who knew that a treat could cause chaos for all?

With stockings a-dangling, I search high and low,
For gifts that aren't socks—what a horrible show!
A broccoli sweater would surely offend,
But who could resist my sweet cat as a friend?

The laughter around me, it sparkles like gold,
When Grandma sings carols, the stories unfold.
To dance with the mismatched, is truly a gift,
As we twirl through the memories, our hearts start to lift.

So let's raise our mugs, with hot cocoa galore,
And toast to the fun—who could want any more?
With flickering embers, our hearts start to gleam,
In this joyous mayhem, we live out the dream.

Starlit Wishes and Cozy Corners

In the nook by the window, a cozy retreat,
I ponder the wishes that fill me with heat.
A scarf too tight, now I'm stuck in my chair,
And no, I don't care if I still have to wear!

The stars start to giggle, they wink from afar,
Like wishes in disguise, a celestial bazaar.
I throw out my troubles, they flutter away,
A comet of humor, come brighten my day!

With hot pies in the oven, a smell so divine,
The cat in the kitchen wishes he could dine.
But alas, he's our jester, the clown of the bunch,
As we laugh at his antics, we all love his crunch!

So gather 'round, friends, in this laughter-filled nest,
With stories and dreams, we find joy in the jest.
As starlit wishes twinkle, and cozy hearts beam,
We cherish these moments, a warm, silly dream.

Snowflakes Dance on the Hearth

Snowflakes tumble, land on the cat,
They wiggle and dance, then fall flat.
Hot cocoa spills, a s'more takes flight,
Who knew the treats could spark such delight?

The dog leaps up, chasing the cheer,
As snowmen giggle, they seem so near.
Mittens hang low, full of marshmallow fluff,
We laugh and we cheer, never can get enough!

The fire is crackling, we toast all the snacks,
Fortified laughter, no one relaxes.
The cat in the tree looks down with a frown,
These snowflakes are winning; let's not let them down!

Pudding is jiggling, it starts to roll,
Right off the table—oh boy, what a goal!
Catch it, don't drop it, the game's now in play,
Just another wild, merry winter's ballet!

Embracing Warmth Amidst the Chill

Fluffy socks dance on the cold wooden floor,
As chirpy birds bundle and clatter at the door.
The kettle sings sweetly, the biscuits adorn,
We brave the cold in our fun, cozy swarm.

Neighbors are shouting in snowball debates,
While the cats plan heists from their warm little states.
The smell of burnt toast wafts through the air,
Laughing together at oven's mishare!

Grandma knits loudly with yarn in fine cheer,
Every loop a sonnet, every stitch crystal clear.
We plot our next heist for the candy jar prize,
As cocoa-sugar gremlins dance with surprise.

The snowman is grumpy, his nose out of place,
While our jolly old snowball war finds its grace.
We hold onto warmth as the evening drifts slow,
The laughter is won, in this winter's tableau!

Tinsel Dreams in Glimmering Shadows

Tinsel twinkles on the tree so bright,
It wiggles and sparkles, a tree's favorite sight.
Shiny baubles roll, making their ruckus,
As we dive for the cookies, the chaos becomes luminous!

The cat on the mantle, all nice and reposed,
Dreams of grand feasts while the turkey's exposed.
We giggle and snicker as we pass him the treats,
Leaping over puddles of mustache-shaped sweets!

A gift-wrapped surprise, what could it be?
A clever old prank or a sock full of glee?
The truth unravels as we scramble and play,
Who knew tinsel dreams could throw us this way?

The night hums with laughter, each twinkling star,
Reflecting our shenanigans from afar.
In our quirky slice of this magical scene,
We dance and we jiggle, all stuffed with whipped cream!

Hearthbound Hopes and Tales

Around the hearth, tales start to roam,
With playful intent, we make quite the dome.
Grandpa spins yarns 'bout his younger days,
While we wink at the fire in a wibbly gaze.

A marshmallow mountain we start to create,
Competing for glory—it's a sticky fate!
The chocolate river spills over the edge,
As we scheme to build our treat-laden pledge.

The dog thinks he's winning with crumbs on his snout,
While the cat plots revenge, swift tail in a pout.
With whiffs of burnt cookies, our dreams stay ablaze,
Laughter erupts in this whimsical maze!

So gather 'round closely, let stories unfold,
As hearts filled with laughter replace winter's cold.
In a world all aglow, our hopes take a flight,
Each memory a snowflake, drifting into the night!

Hearthbound Memories

The turkey's done, or so they claim,
But Uncle Joe just played the game.
He took a nap, he had a snack,
And now he's snoring on the stack.

The lights are tangled, what a sight,
The cat has found a new delight.
He swats at bulbs, with gleeful cheer,
And we all hold our breath in fear.

A dance contest breaks out in glee,
With grandma busting moves so free.
An elbow hits the punch bowl, splash!
And now our party's quite the crash!

Yet through the mess and all the cheer,
These crazy moments bring us near.
So grab a mug and raise a toast,
To family, fun, we love the most!

Radiance Amidst the Frost

The snowflakes twirl like ballerinas,
While dad brings out his wacky zucchinis.
Decorations fly, a tape measure's fate,
As mom adorns, oh what a state!

The cookie dough's in quite a stew,
With sprinkles flying, red and blue.
And when we bake, the smoke alarms,
Join in the fun with loud alarms!

The reindeer stand on rooftops high,
But one has landed, oh my, oh my!
He munches treats left in a bowl,
The neighbor's cat gives him a scowl.

Yet laughter rings as we all share,
These silly tales beyond compare.
So let the frost swirl all around,
Our laughter's warmth is truly found!

A Tapestry of Yuletide Dreams

The tree's ablaze with lights so bright,
While siblings squabble in pure delight.
Who eats the cookies? It's always a fight,
As parents just shake their heads at the sight.

The elf on the shelf has lost its way,
It's up on the fridge, what a display!
While grandpa tells tales that we've heard before,
Of Santa's sleigh crashing at the door.

Nana's fruitcake is quite the treat,
It bounces well, but we can't eat.
Yet still we laugh and share the cheer,
For every bite brings us near.

With socks hung high and hopes in sight,
We gather close on this joyful night.
So let us spin tales around the fire,
With giggles and dreams that never tire!

Fireside Flickers of Joy

The crackling fire pops and sings,
While underfoot a puppy clings.
He nibbles on the ornaments bright,
Creating chaos, pure delight!

The cocoa's spilled with marshmallows galore,
Kids wrestle lightly on the floor.
And who will find the hidden gift?
It's like a treasure hunt with a twist!

The carols played, out of tune,
Yet we all dance under the moon.
Dad tries to sing, we hold our side,
As laughter echoes, oh what a ride!

So gather round, let joy ignite,
With silly stories to share tonight.
For memories made are the greatest treasure,
Wrapped in laughter, love, and pure pleasure!

The Scent of Pine and Promise

The tree's a bit lopsided, oh dear,
But the lights keep on blinking with cheer.
Garlands are tangled, like a cat's play,
Yet the cocoa tastes better that way!

Snowflakes are falling, a fluffy white coat,
I thought I could ski—oh, I hope I don't float.
My snowman's in trouble, he's melting away,
Guess I'll just have to make a new play!

The cookies are burnt, but who's keeping score?
We laugh until we can't take it anymore.
With friends all around, what more do we need?
Just laughter, and sugar, and lots of good greed!

So here's to the season, with cheer and with sass,
Full of giggles and blunders, none of us pass.
Let's raise a hot mug and toast to our crew,
May each silly moment bring joy to renew!

Stars Above and Hearts Alight

The stars blink and twinkle, like eyes in the night,
While the dog barks at darkness, oh what a sight!
We're bundled in blankets, with cocoa in hand,
Discussing our plans for a snowball fight grand!

Lights on the roof seem to twinkle and sway,
The neighbors just wonder how we'll be okay.
We giggle at elves, who just might drop by,
With a sleigh full of mischief—oh my, oh my!

Our ham's on the table, but smells like a sock,
While the turkey is shouting, "Hey, don't you mock!"
We munch on the failings, with spirits so bright,
Finding laughter in chaos, that feels just so right!

So let's deck the halls with a little more cheer,
With memories made, and good friends ever near.
Together we dance, in this twinkling delight,
Under stars that remind us of dreams taking flight!

Embracing the Chill with Open Arms

Jack Frost's been nipping like a playful fool,
But we'll start a fire and follow the rule:
To toast marshmallows while singing a tune,
Distracting the howl of the cold winter moon.

A snowball flies past—oh, it's a surprise,
From a cheeky little child with mischievous eyes.
We're dodging and weaving, a dance in white fluff,
Until icy fingers remind us—enough!

The frostbite's creeping, we retreat to our lair,
With blankets and stories that float through the air.
We share our blunders and giggle with glee,
As we sip on some cider, and argue on key!

So here's to the chilly, with its infinite charm,
That keeps us together, all cozy and warm.
We laugh through the frost, with our hearts all aglow,
Finding joy in the winter, come rain, sleet, or snow!

Together in the Warmth of Remembrance

Gathered around, we recount how it's been,
Our childhood adventures, oh where to begin?
The time we made poppers and set them ablaze,
Still chuckling about those hilarious days!

The stockings are hung, with care and a laugh,
And uncle Joe swears he knows the best craft.
The tree's a reminder of years full of cheer,
As moments and memories wrap us all near.

We hold up our mugs, sharing stories that glow,
Of relatives goofy, who didn't quite know.
With warmth in our hearts and sparkles in eyes,
Laughter's the secret, that's never a surprise!

So let's raise a toast to the jokes that we share,
To bonds that grow stronger, that show how we care.
As we gather together, our spirits ignite,
In the glow of remembrance, everything feels right!

Cradled in Comfort and Kindness

In sweaters too tight, we gather 'round,
With cookies aplenty and laughter found.
The dog steals a treat, oh what a sight,
As we munch on the snacks, with pure delight.

The fire is crackling, it pops and it sizzles,
While Uncle Joe tries to avoid all the fizzles.
The jokes are so bad, we're rolling on floors,
Lost in our giggles, forgetting our chores.

The lights twinkle bright, like stars in a race,
While Aunt Margie insists on a dance space.
With moves that are quirky, we sway and we twirl,
In our silly socks, we spin and we whirl.

So here's to the season, where chaos is bliss,
With love in the air and a warm mug to miss.
In comfort we bask, with hearts open wide,
Enjoying the madness, our laughter our guide.

Lullabies for the Frosty Evening

The snow flakes come down, a soft white parade,
While Grandpa snores loudly, his plans all delayed.
A cozy quilt drapes on a chair, oh so near,
With hot cocoa waiting, we have not a fear.

The clock softly chimes, it's time to unwind,
As Grandma recounts how she once lost her mind.
With stories so wild, we giggle and cheer,
Each tale leaves us gasping, we're all of good cheer.

Outside the winds howl, a frosty old tune,
We peek through the window, it's a magical boon.
With marshmallows flying, we cheer from within,
While outside, the neighbors just wish it would thin.

A lullaby hums, as we snuggle up tight,
In dreams filled with candy, the world feels so bright.
With wishes and whispers, we drift off to sleep,
In the glow of the hearth, our secrets we keep.

Festivities Under the Velvet Sky

The stars are all twinkling, can't help but remark,
As Aunt Sally's hat catches fire from the spark.
The laughter erupts, like a pop and a fizz,
While we wave it off, 'till it ends with a whiz.

With tinsel all tangled and garlands askew,
We're stirring up mischief, as families do.
The tree looks a bit like it needs a good friend,
But our hearts shine the brightest, that's how we blend.

We toast to the chaos, our spirits so high,
As mistletoe dangles, and cousins all vie.
With jokes cracking wide as the eggnog spills free,
The night is a tapestry, woven with glee.

Under the velvet sky, we raise up a cheer,
For the moments that bind us, the love that is clear.
In boots that are mismatched, we dance and we play,
As joy hugs us warm, in its magical way.

Festooned Halls and Laughter's Echo

With garlands hung low and the music so bright,
The halls are all decked, it's a magical sight.
But last year's fruitcake lies still in the dark,
While siblings debate who'll take it to park.

The snowmen outside, looking rather forlorn,
As the cat makes a dash through the flurries, they scorn.
Yet here we all gather, in spirits so high,
A buffet of giggles under the sky.

The punch bowl's stocked, but it's fruity and strange,
A concoction that's bound to send taste buds estranged.
Yet we all play along, with our cups raised up high,
Toast to the mayhem, let unity fly!

With laughter's rich echo, we cherish the night,
As stories are shared 'neath the soft candlelight.
The warmth of connection, beyond any prize,
Is wrapped up like presents, a true sweet surprise.

The Serenity of Shared Sighs

In the glow of lights, we chuckle and cheer,
Unwrapping presents and wishing you were here.
The cat's in the tree, what a sight to behold,
While the cookies we baked have all crumbled, and scrolled.

A fruitcake of terror sits proudly on display,
We pretend it's delicious, just to be polite, hey!
Uncle Joe's telling jokes that are older than time,
We all roll our eyes, but it's still quite a rhyme.

The punch bowl is empty, that's quite an odd sign,
As the shadows grow long and the stars start to shine.
We swap all our stories while snickering loud,
These moments together, oh, make us so proud.

As the evening winds down and the laughter gets small,
We bask in the warmth, feeling lucky through all.
With a wink and a grin, we'll turn down the fun,
But tomorrow, we promise, we'll do it, just one!

Beneath the Mistletoe's Embrace

Under the greenery, we giggle and sway,
Stuck in a bunch of peculiar ballet.
The chap with a wink is a friend of good cheer,
But his dance moves need work, that's totally clear.

Lips puckered like fish, oh, the awkward delight,
As the dog snags our snacks, what a comical sight!
We smirk and we poke, saying no thanks to fate,
For the thrill of the kiss with a doubt we create.

A mistletoe sprig dangles high in the room,
Where romances begin, or they just meet their doom.
With each clumsy twirl, we share hearty laughs,
As our hearts skip a beat, in absolute gaffs.

So here's to shared kisses that might not align,
Next time we'll plan it, oh boy! We all chime.
But for now, let's just hope that it all brings good cheer,
As we toast to the nights full of fun and good beer!

Savoring Wishes on the Wind

A snowman stands tall with a lopsided grin,
His carrot nose crooked, let the mischief begin!
As snowflakes keep falling, we giggle with glee,
Our dreams floating around like a frosty balloon tree.

The stockings hang low, but one fell on the fire,
It melted to mush, oh, the chaos—desired!
We laugh and we talk 'bout the things we hold dear,
Like that time cousin Tim tripped and fell in the beer.

Wishes on the wind, swirling bright through the air,
Each one a giggle, with laughter to spare.
With nonsense discussed, how we long for those days,
When we raised our voices in the silliest ways.

So let's share our wishes, both funny and bright,
With prankish intentions that dance through the night.
Embracing the joy that together we find,
In moments of laughter, our hearts all aligned!

Frosted Windowpanes and Heartfelt Rhymes

Frosted windowpanes frame a scene full of cheer,
As we peek at our neighbors, what's really unclear?
They're dancing a jig, with a turkey on high,
While we polish our spoons, oh why not? Let's try!

The aroma of fudge wafts in meandering ways,
Uncle Bob's kitchen antics—oh, the culinary plays!
We stir and we mix while we plot and we scheme,
To prank Auntie May with our goofy team dream.

So here's to the laughter that cozy nights bring,
While we craft silly rhymes meant to make our hearts sing.
The warmth of these moments, our joy intertwined,
In the bustle and chaos, true happiness we find.

When the clock strikes the hour, and we say our goodnights,
We'll remember these giggles, fond memories in sights.
Through frosted windowpanes, we send out delight,
As we clink in our cups, let's toast to the night!

The Glow of Togetherness

Around the fire, socks are tossed,
Hot cocoa spills, we're at a loss.
The dog steals cookies, oh what a sight,
While Uncle Bob dances with delight.

Laughter erupts with each silly joke,
As Grandma challenges us—who will poke?
With twinkling lights strung way too low,
We tripped on cords, oh what a show!

Mismatched PJs on the family crew,
Elf hats askew, but we don't mind, do?
The cat on the mantel, what a grand pose,
As reindeer fly past with squeaky nose!

Fudge on the table, but who can resist?
With recipes shared, gave the chefs a twist.
In our cuddly chaos, we all agree,
This merry gathering is pure jubilee.

Starlit Evenings and Joyful Refrains

Beneath the stars with a wink and a cheer,
We sing off-key, but we have no fear.
A carrot for snowmen, our lips all a-chatter,
While squirrels join in, like it really matters!

The mistletoe hangs, awkward and stuck,
A peck from the grandpa who's just out of luck!
While penguin-shaped cookies crumble in hand,
We giggle and snack—oh, isn't it grand?

Snowball fights break into spontaneous dance,
With snowflakes that seem to giggle and prance.
Hot cider is sipped with a splash of good cheer,
As we shout "I love this" while friends disappear!

With jest and with laughter, we bid the night,
As socks on the radiator bring warmth so bright.
The glow of our moments, a spark in our soul,
We wish every day had a similar goal.

Echoes of Laughter in Snowy Silence

In frosty whispers, the shadows creep,
As snowmen stand guard, all stoic—and steep.
We flung snowballs wildly, laughter on blast,
Yet somehow, that one hit Dad—what a cast!

Around the table, bad jokes take flight,
With cousins as jesters, oh what a night!
The punch bowl's a treasure, but spilled on the floor,
As everyone giggles, and begs for some more.

Chasing the dog with a wrap in hand,
Dressed like a present, he doesn't quite stand.
Squeaky toys scatter, the new favorite join,
As Aunt Sally's stories you can't quite conjoin!

Yet through all the mayhem, the gifts jumbled tight,
We hold to the warmth 'til the morning light.
For in silly moments, connections are made,
We grasp our togetherness, never to fade.

A Tapestry of Tradition and Light

Threads of some tinsel hang from the wall,
As chaotic relatives come for the haul.
With stories retold and laughter so loud,
We sometimes forget there's a time to be proud.

With lanterns that flicker and candles that sway,
Sharing our secrets in the porch's gray.
An ornament lost: was it blue? Was it red?
We all have our tales of things that we dread!

The cat tree's adorned like a sad little prize,
With feathers and bows, oh how it belies!
Yet somehow we gather to drink in the cheer,
In our tangled-up harmony, our hearts draw near.

And as the night fades into soft, velvet dreams,
We cling to the silliness lost in our schemes.
For in the delight of these whimsical hours,
We build a warm fortress that no one devours!

Candles Flicker in Timeless Treasures

Candles flicker, shadows dance,
Granny's recipe, a clumsy chance.
Gingerbread men with arms askew,
Frosting mishaps, oh, what a view!

The tree is lopsided, ornaments fall,
Uncle Joe's snoring, can we hear it all?
A cat on the mantle, claiming it too,
With each goofy grin, our laughter grew.

Grandpa's stories, a twist here and there,
Of how he lost his prized teddy bear.
With jokes that land, and others that flop,
The joy in the air makes heartbeats pop!

So here's to the mess, the giggles and glee,
In moments like this, we find our spree.
Candles burn bright, laughter's the thread,
In this warm chaos, love is well fed.

Stories Told by Flickering Flame

By the flickering flame, we gather round,
Tales of Aunt Mabel's dog, profound.
Who chased after turkey, took quite a leap,
And made the whole feast turn into a heap!

Uncle Mike's jokes, a few fits of clamor,
We laugh and we groan at his wild grammar.
A snowman with style in a hat way too wide,
He slid down the hill with a graceless glide.

The lights overhead twinkle, oh what a sight,
While Cousin Sue's dessert is a horrible fright.
It wobbled and jiggled like jelly gone rogue,
We all took a taste, and it felt like a joke!

So let's raise a toast to what makes us whole,
With mismatched socks and laughter that rolls.
We'll tell stories by flame till the night becomes late,
In the warm joys of life, we just celebrate!

The Blessing of Togetherness and Cheer

Gather round the table, it's quite a sight,
We've got half-baked casseroles and soda pop light.
The dog in a sweater, though it fits too tight,
He steals all the biscuits, and oh, what a bite!

Mom's got her apron, but it's quite a mess,
With flour on her face, she's making a guess.
We argue and chuckle, it's part of the plan,
'Cause nothing's quite right without Uncle Stan.

The gifts all wrapped, some too big to hide,
A box of mismatched socks? What a wild ride!
With giggles and pokes, we dive into cheer,
Overcooked veggies? We'll still persevere!

So come one, come all, to this joyful parade,
With laughter and love, our worries do fade.
We're not perfect, it's true, but who wants that fuss?
In the warmth of each other, it's all a big plus!

Emotions Kindled Beneath the Boughs

Beneath the boughs, emotions run high,
As the cat steals the gift from the tree standing by.
The wrappings flutter like a wild parade,
And Dad's face turns red when the dog makes a raid!

With laughter we gather, a chorus so bright,
Rehashing old times, till we giggle at night.
A snowball fight started before dessert's served,
Leaving plates piled high and laughter preserved!

We tease Aunt Linda, her holiday hat,
With ornaments glittering, perched like a cat.
In tales that we tell, the silly and sweet,
Our hearts all come home, in joy we repeat.

So here's to this madness, the winks and the cheers,
In this cozy retreat, we conquer our fears.
With each quirky moment, and silly good cheer,
We'll cherish forever, this time spent right here.

The Magic in a Gathered Glow

A roast so big, it takes the floor,
The dog escapes, he's back for more!
Pine needles stick to all the chairs,
As laughter fills the cozy lairs.

Uncle Joe attempts a dance so spry,
But trips on tinsel, oh my my!
The kids are giggling, covered in pie,
While grandma's knitting something awry.

We light the candles, one, two, three,
Then knock them over; oh, could it be?
A flame ignites our joyful scream,
As we realize it was all a dream!

Yet through the chaos, smiles take flight,
In our warm home, it feels just right.
Though sparks may fly and cheese might clump,
Love wraps us up, a fluffy lump.

Songs of the Season

The carolers sing off-key tonight,
And everyone joins in, what a sight!
The cat jumps high, knocking the tree,
As we belt out the tunes, all carefree.

A chorus of laughter fills the air,
With mom cracking jokes, a real flair!
Dad's forgotten the words yet again,
But he'll just hum and start over then.

A pot of soup overflows with cheer,
As Aunt Sue claims she'll bring more this year.
The music's loud, the dancing too,
Even the dog joins in, woohoo!

So we gather around, our voices blend,
With silly songs, the fun won't end.
Each note a memory, merry and bright,
As we hold on tight to this joyful night.

Softly Shared

The cookies disappear, a sneaky hand,
The kids are plotting, a crumb-filled band.
Chocolate stains on the best tablecloth,
But giggles replace any form of wrath.

We swap our tales, both wild and true,
Of gingerbread men that almost flew.
A gift wrapped tight but filled with socks,
As dad unpacks it, we all just mock.

The glow of lights with a flicker here,
And grandma's knitting, a holiday cheer.
Each shared moment, a quirky delight,
Making memories that feel just right.

So as we gather on this fine eve,
With joyful hearts, we truly believe.
In laughter and love, our spirits soar,
Creating magic that we'll all adore.

Illuminated Pathways Homeward

The streets aglow with bulbs and cheer,
As we stumble home, with pies we veer.
Uncle Phil's sleigh, oh how it sways,
While singing loudly in crazy ways.

The snowflakes tickle as we run,
With each step forward, it's all pure fun.
A snowman made that looks quite round,
Till the neighbor's dog rolls it around.

With hot cocoa made by little hands,
Mug spills over; oh, how it stands!
We sip and smile, wrapping up tight,
As joyful laughter fills the night.

And every stumble, each joyful slip,
Just makes us laugh harder on this trip.
With memories bright and pathways bold,
We treasure these times, worth more than gold.

A Wreath of Memories and Miracles

The wreath is crooked, hung with glee,
While puppy tags at it, oh what a spree!
Mom's out of breath, she's lost the fight,
Still dusting off twinkly lights so bright.

In mismatched socks, dad leads the pack,
Tripping over the gifts, he turns back.
"Every box wrapped with love," he'll claim,
As we tease him softly with gentle aim.

The tree's a bit tilted, but who can tell?
It holds our laughter, and that's just swell.
With stories shared around the glow,
Each moment cherished, in hearts we stow.

So here we gather, both far and near,
With tales and quirks, we hold so dear.
Crafting memories, each silly cheer,
In our wreath of love, year after year.